Goose on the Loose

By Clem King

T0360247

Dirk the goose was hungry.

The smell of a yummy pie came from the house.

Dirk kicked his food.

"I don't want this goop,"
he said.

Dirk walked to the side
of his pen.

"If I get on the roof
of the coop, I can jump out,"
he said.
"And get the pie!"

Dirk swooped off the roof!

The hens got a big fright.

The hungry goose went into the house.

The pie was in the room.

Dirk scoffed as much pie as he could!

Soon, Nan came in with Bert.

They looked at Dirk.

Dirk looked at them.

Pie oozed from his beak.

"The goose is loose!"
yelled Nan.
"Get the broom!"

"Shoo! Shoo, you silly goose!" yelled Bert.

Dirk scooped up the pie dish.

He zoomed out of the house!

"Dirk has my pie!" yelled Nan.

Dirk ran into the pond.

The broom could not
get to him!

Nan was in a bad mood.

"That pie was for you,
Bert," said Nan.

Dirk ate the rest of the pie.

He was **so** happy, he swam loops in the pond.

The moon came out.

Nan and Bert went to bed.

Dirk swam and swam.

"Gosh, I love pie!" he said.

CHECKING FOR MEANING

1. What could Dirk smell coming from the house? *(Literal)*

2. What did Bert do to get Dirk out of the house? *(Literal)*

3. Why did Dirk eat as much of the pie as he could when he was in the house? *(Inferential)*

EXTENDING VOCABULARY

goop	What is *goop*? How would you describe goop? Is it gooey, slimy, crispy, crunchy?
scooped	What does *scooped* mean? Which part of his body did Dirk use to scoop up the pie? What other words could replace *scooped* in this sentence without changing the meaning? *Dirk scooped up the pie dish.* E.g. picked, lifted, bundled.
zoomed	What does *zoomed* mean? Did Dirk move quickly or slowly with the pie? What other words do you know that have a similar meaning? E.g. whizzed, zipped, whooshed.

MOVING BEYOND THE TEXT

1. Which foods do you like the smell of when they are cooked or cooking?

2. What plants do you know that have a strong smell?

3. What other words do you know that mean the same as *smell*? E.g. perfume, aroma, odour.

4. If you were Bert, what would you have done to get the pie from Dirk?

SPEED SOUNDS

oo	ue	ew	ui	u_e

ou	u	oe	o

PRACTICE WORDS

goose

food

goop

roof

coop

swooped

into

oozed

room

Soon

zoomed

Shoo

broom

loose

Hoot

mood

to

scooped

moon

loops

you